T0400825

DALLAS STARS

BY HAROLD P. CAIN

Copyright © 2023 by Press Room Editions. All rights reserved. No part of this book may be used or reproduced in any manner whatsoever, including internet usage, without written permission from the copyright owner, except in the case of brief quotations embodied in critical articles and reviews.

Book design by Maggie Villaume
Cover design by Maggie Villaume

Photographs ©: Jeffrey McWhorter/AP Images, cover; Jason Franson/The Canadian Press/AP Images, 4–5, 7, 9; Melchior DiGiacomo/Getty Images, 10–11; Harry Harris/AP Images, 13; Fred Jewell/AP Images, 15; Mark J. Terrill/AP Images, 16–17; LM Otero/AP Images, 18–19; Ryan Remiorz/CAP Images, 21; Icon Sports Media, 23; Ray Carlin/Icon Sportswire, 24–25; Jeanine Leech/Icon Sportswire, 27; Matthew Pearce/Icon Sportswire, 29

Press Box Books, an imprint of Press Room Editions.

ISBN
978-1-63494-490-8 (library bound)
978-1-63494-516-5 (paperback)
978-1-63494-567-7 (epub)
978-1-63494-542-4 (hosted ebook)

Library of Congress Control Number: 2022902270

Distributed by North Star Editions, Inc.
2297 Waters Drive
Mendota Heights, MN 55120
www.northstareditions.com

Printed in the United States of America
082022

ABOUT THE AUTHOR

Harold P. Cain is a retired English teacher and lifelong sports fan originally from Rockford, Illinois. He and his wife now live in Cathedral City, California, where they enjoy hiking, golf, and spending time with their daughter and three grandchildren in Los Angeles.

TABLE OF CONTENTS

CHAPTER 1
HEADING TO THE FINAL
5

CHAPTER 2
NORTHERN ROOTS
11

CHAPTER 3
LONE STAR STATE
17

SUPERSTAR PROFILE
MIKE MODANO
22

CHAPTER 4
A NEW ERA
25

QUICK STATS	30
GLOSSARY	31
TO LEARN MORE	32
INDEX	32

1

Dallas Stars forward Denis Gurianov attempts a shot during Game 5 of the 2020 Conference Final.

HEADING TO THE FINAL

Dallas Stars center Tyler Seguin glided toward the goal. Suddenly a pass slid toward him from behind the net. Seguin fired a shot. But the goalie made a kick save, and the puck bounced away.

A goal would have tied the game. However, the Stars still trailed 1–0 early in the third period. Dallas was facing the Vegas

Golden Knights in Game 5 of the 2020 Conference Final. The Stars led the series three games to one. And they wanted to end the series right here.

The Golden Knights gained control of the puck and started heading the other way. A Vegas player fired a shot past Stars goalie Anton Khudobin. The Golden Knights now led 2–0.

The Stars had a lot of work to do. But they didn't panic. Halfway through the

JUST ENOUGH OFFENSE

The Stars didn't score many goals during the 2019–20 season. In fact, they scored the third fewest in the league. Denis Gurianov led the team with only 20. However, Dallas did have a balanced scoring attack when it came to total points. Jamie Benn led the team with 50 points. Six other players had 30 or more.

Stars goalie Anton Khudobin defends the net against the Vegas Golden Knights.

third period, Dallas left winger Jamie Benn collected a rebound in front of the goal. He shot it past the Vegas goalie to cut the lead in half. Like Seguin, Benn was one of the team's top players. But it would take a team effort if Dallas was going to complete the comeback.

The Stars got a big break when they went on a power play later in the period. Veteran Corey Perry skated in front of the net. He helped create a rebound for forward Joel Kiviranta, who stuffed home the tying goal. The 24-year-old Kiviranta was a rookie. He had played in only 11 games during the regular season.

The Stars held on to force overtime. Just a few minutes into the extra period, they got another power play. John Klingberg passed the puck to rookie Denis Gurianov. Gurianov blasted a powerful one-timer into the back of the net. The Stars had won the series! Now they were headed to the Stanley Cup Final.

Stars forward Joel Kiviranta celebrates his third-period goal against the Vegas Golden Knights.

2

North Stars captain Ted Harris prepares to take a face-off in the early 1970s.

NORTHERN ROOTS

For many years, the National Hockey League (NHL) was made up of just six teams. But in 1967, the league doubled in size. The Minnesota North Stars were one of six new teams. Fans in the hockey-crazy state eagerly embraced their team. They were even treated to a playoff run. The North Stars upset the Los Angeles Kings in the first round.

The North Stars were a regular playoff team in their early years. Winger Bill Goldsworthy proved to be a goal-scoring machine. He had five seasons with 30 or more goals. Goalie Gump Worsley came out of retirement to play for the North Stars. The former Vezina Trophy winner provided a veteran presence in net. Meanwhile, defenseman Ted Harris served

BILL MASTERTON

In the North Stars' first season, center Bill Masterton died after hitting his head on the ice. He is the only player in NHL history to die from an injury suffered in a game. Helmets were optional at the time. But by 1979, they were required for all new players. The NHL also created the Bill Masterton Memorial Trophy. It is awarded each year to a player who shows great sportsmanship.

North Stars goalie Pete Lopresti defends the net during a 1977 game against the New York Islanders.

as the team's captain. He could shut down opposing goal scorers.

The North Stars ended the 1970s on a string of losing seasons. Then in 1981, Minnesota native Neal Broten arrived. He joined the North Stars just in time for the team's surprising run to the 1981 Stanley Cup Final. Unfortunately for North Stars fans, the New York Islanders won the series in five games.

In 1991, second-year center Mike Modano carried Minnesota to another Stanley Cup Final. The North Stars even led the series two games to one. But then they dropped three straight games. The Pittsburgh Penguins ended up winning the title.

In the early 1990s, the North Stars had poor attendance at their games. Owner Norm Green believed Minnesota needed a new arena to bring in more fans. However, he couldn't get local leaders to build one. So, in 1993, Green decided to

North Stars left winger Basil McRae attempts a shot against the Chicago Blackhawks in 1990.

move the team to Texas. They dropped the word "North" from their name and became the Dallas Stars.

3

Stars right winger Jere Lehtinen takes the puck down the ice during a 1996 matchup with the Mighty Ducks of Anaheim.

LONE STAR STATE

The Stars were part of an NHL trend in the 1990s. The league was expanding into parts of North America that had never had pro hockey before. There weren't many hockey fans in Dallas when the Stars arrived in 1993. But the team won a lot. And that was something any sports fan could enjoy.

A sellout crowd welcomed the Stars in their first home game. The team gave the Texas fans plenty to cheer for. Dallas beat the Detroit Red Wings 6–4.

The team's top players from that era included Mike Modano and Derian Hatcher. Modano went on to become one of the greatest American-born players in history. Meanwhile, Hatcher brought physical play and leadership.

Dallas added other talented players around them. Goalie Ed Belfour already had two Vezina Trophies under his belt when he joined the Stars. Center Joe Nieuwendyk brought 30-goal potential.

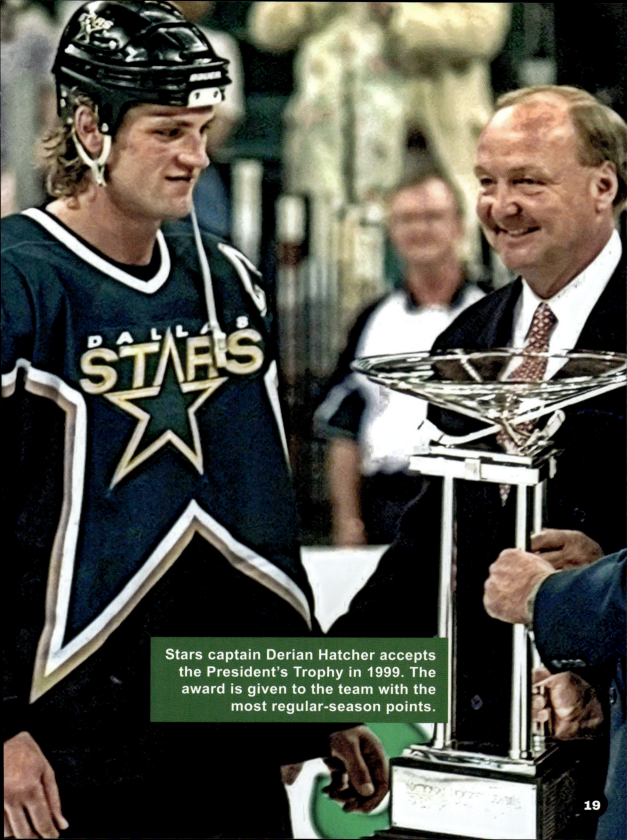

Stars captain Derian Hatcher accepts the President's Trophy in 1999. The award is given to the team with the most regular-season points.

Before the 1998–99 season started, Dallas signed superstar Brett Hull. He was the final piece of the puzzle on a talented team. In 1999, the Stars made it to the Stanley Cup Final for the first time in their new city. And in triple overtime of Game 6, Hull scored the Cup-winning goal. The Stars were champions!

Dallas nearly pulled off a repeat. However, they lost the 2000 Final to the

•THE WINNING GOAL

Brett Hull's winning goal in the 1999 Stanley Cup Final was thrilling for Stars fans. But not everyone was happy. Many people thought the goal shouldn't have counted. One of Hull's skates was in the crease when he made the shot. As far as players and fans knew, that wasn't allowed. However, the NHL had secretly changed the rule earlier in the season. So, Hull's goal counted.

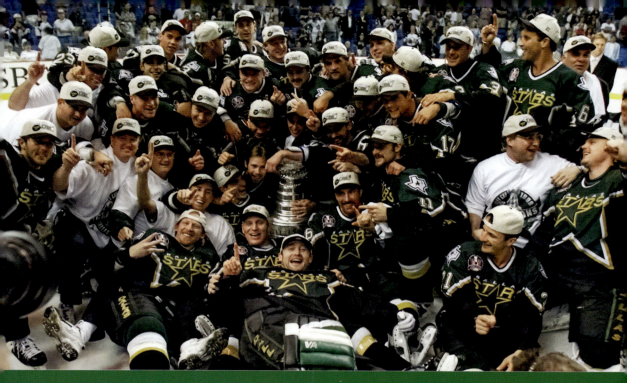

The Stars pose for a team photo after winning the 1999 Stanley Cup.

New Jersey Devils. Players like Hull and Nieuwendyk left soon after the Cup years. But Modano and Hatcher stuck around for several more seasons. They helped mentor the next generation. Marty Turco took over for Belfour in the net. And on offense, Brenden Morrow became the team's next big goal scorer.

● SUPERSTAR PROFILE

MIKE MODANO

Mike Modano burst onto the scene as a 19-year-old rookie in 1989. His smooth skating and powerful shots dazzled fans in Minnesota. He also put up impressive numbers. In his rookie season, Modano recorded 29 goals and 75 total points.

Modano continued to improve after the Stars moved to Dallas. He put together a 50-goal season in 1993–94. Modano also developed into an excellent two-way forward. Teammates appreciated his effort on both offense and defense. Fans loved him, too. Modano's jersey was one of the top sellers in Dallas throughout his career.

In 2007, Modano made American hockey history. He scored the 503rd goal of his career. That passed Joe Mullen for most goals by an American-born player. Later in the year, Modano passed Phil Housley for the most points by an American.

Modano finished his Hall of Fame career with 561 goals and 813 assists.

4

Jamie Benn led the NHL in points in the 2014–15 season.

A NEW ERA

By 2013, the Stars had missed the playoffs five years in a row. But plenty of changes were in store for the team. For instance, forward Jamie Benn was named captain. Benn was only in his fifth NHL season. Even so, he was already one of Dallas's top goal scorers.

Dallas also traded for Tyler Seguin. The talented forward was just 21 years old. He had already scored 56 goals in 203 career games. Seguin and Benn were the team's top scorers in 2013–14. Best of all, they led Dallas back to the playoffs.

In 2016, the Stars won their first playoff series in nearly a decade. However, the team still struggled to compete for a championship. As the 2019–20 season was nearing its end, the team was headed in the wrong direction. The Stars seemed unlikely to even reach the playoffs.

Then in March 2020, the COVID-19 pandemic put a stop to the season. Months later, the season started up again. The Stars automatically made the playoffs. And suddenly, Dallas got hot.

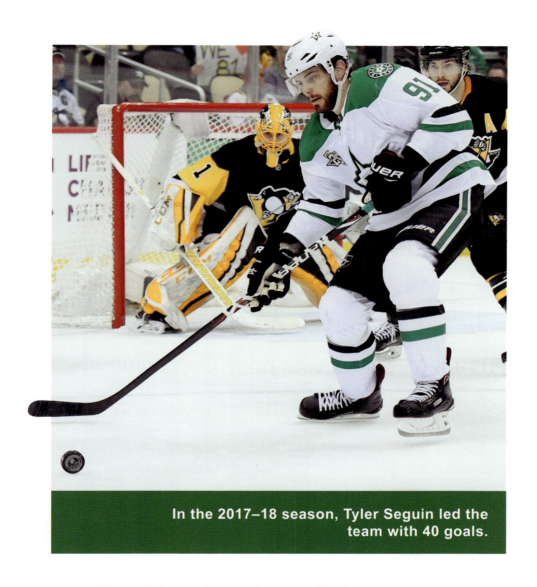

In the 2017–18 season, Tyler Seguin led the team with 40 goals.

The Stars knocked off the Calgary Flames in the first round. Then they defeated the Colorado Avalanche in the second. After that, Dallas beat the Golden Knights with an incredible overtime victory. That sent the Stars back to the Stanley Cup Final for the first time in years.

Dallas ended up losing the Final to the Tampa Bay Lightning. Still, the surprising run was thrilling to watch. And with several young stars on the rise, fans hoped the team would lift the Stanley Cup again soon.

WARM WINTER CLASSIC

The Stars hosted the Winter Classic in 2020. This game is played outdoors every January 1. Dallas doesn't have cold winters, so the game was the warmest Winter Classic in history. The temperature stood at 55 degrees Fahrenheit (13°C). The game also drew one of the largest crowds in NHL history. More than 85,000 fans packed into the Cotton Bowl to watch the action.

Dallas goalie Ben Bishop makes a save during the 2020 Winter Classic.

DALLAS STARS QUICK STATS

TEAM HISTORY: Minnesota North Stars (1967–1993), Dallas Stars (1993–)

STANLEY CUP CHAMPIONSHIPS: 1 (1999)

KEY COACHES:
- Ken Hitchcock (1996–2002, 2017–18): 319 wins, 186 losses, 60 ties, 20 overtime losses
- Dave Tippett (2003–09): 271 wins, 156 losses, 28 ties, 37 overtime losses

HOME ARENA: American Airlines Center (Dallas, TX)

MOST CAREER POINTS: Mike Modano (1,359)

MOST CAREER GOALS: Mike Modano (557)

MOST CAREER ASSISTS: Mike Modano (802)

MOST CAREER SHUTOUTS: Marty Turco (40)

*Stats are accurate through the 2020–21 season.

GLOSSARY

CAPTAIN
A team's leader.

CONFERENCE
A subset of teams within a sports league.

CREASE
The area directly in front of the goalie, painted in blue.

ONE-TIMER
A shot that a player takes immediately after receiving a pass, without controlling the puck first.

PLAYOFFS
A set of games to decide a league's champion.

ROOKIE
A professional athlete in his or her first year of competition.

SPORTSMANSHIP
The act of treating opponents with respect and playing by the rules.

VETERAN
A player who has spent several years in a league.

VEZINA TROPHY
The NHL's annual award for best goaltender.

TO LEARN MORE

BOOKS

Davidson, B. Keith. *NHL*. New York: Crabtree Publishing Company, 2022.

McCabe, Matthew. *It's Great to Be a Fan in Texas*. Lake Elmo, MN: Focus Readers, 2019.

Williamson, Ryan. *NHL Hot Streaks*. Mankato, MN: The Child's World, 2019.

MORE INFORMATION

To learn more about the Dallas Stars, go to **pressboxbooks.com/AllAccess**.

These links are routinely monitored and updated to provide the most current information available.

INDEX

Belfour, Ed, 18, 21
Benn, Jamie, 6–7, 25–26
Broten, Neal, 13

Goldsworthy, Bill, 12
Green, Norm, 14
Gurianov, Denis, 6, 8

Harris, Ted, 12
Hatcher, Derian, 18, 21
Hull, Brett, 20–21

Khudobin, Anton, 6
Kiviranta, Joel, 8
Klingberg, John, 8

Masterton, Bill, 12
Minnesota North Stars, 11–15
Modano, Mike, 14, 18, 21, 22
Morrow, Brenden, 21

Nieuwendyk, Joe, 18, 21

Perry, Corey, 8

Seguin, Tyler, 5, 7, 25–26

Turco, Marty, 21

Worsley, Gump, 12